SHAKER LIGHT

Books by Robert Peters

Poetry

FOURTEEN POEMS
SONGS FOR A SON
THE SOW'S HEAD AND OTHER POEMS
EIGHTEEN POEMS
BYRON EXHUMED
RED MIDNIGHT MOON
CONNECTIONS: In the English Lake District
HOLY COW: Parable Poems
COOL ZEBRAS OF LIGHT
BRONCHIAL TANGLE, HEART SYSTEM
THE GIFT TO BE SIMPLE: A Garland for Ann Lee Founder of the Shakers
THE POET AS ICE-SKATER
GAUGUIN'S CHAIR: Selected Poems
HAWTHORNE
THE DROWNED MAN TO THE FISH
CELEBRITIES: In Memory of Margaret Dumont
THE PICNIC IN THE SNOW: Ludwig II of Bavaria
IKAGNAK
LUDWIG: The Acting Version
THE BLOOD COUNTESS: The Acting Version
WHAT DILLINGER MEANT TO ME
HAWKER
KANE
THE BLOOD COUNTESS: Poems and a Play

Criticism

THE CROWNS OF APOLLO: Swinburne's Principles of Literature and Art
PIONEERS OF MODERN POETRY (with George Hitchcock)
THE GREAT AMERICAN POETRY BAKE-OFF: First, Second, and Third Series
THE PETERS BLACK AND BLUE GUIDES TO CURRENT LITERARY
   PERIODICALS: First, Second and Third Series

Editions

THE POETS NOW SERIES OF LIVING AMERICAN POETS: Scarecrow Press
THE LETTERS OF JOHN ADDINGTON SYMONDS (with Herbert Schueller)

Robert Peters

SHAKER LIGHT

MOTHER ANN LEE IN AMERICA

1987

Greensboro: Unicorn Press, Inc.

Some of these poems have appeared previously in the following periodicals and are reprinted with the kind permission of their editors:

BACHY, EAST RIVER REVIEW, HANDBOOK, POETRY NOW, and YANKEE.

Assistance for the publication of this edition was received from the National Endowment for the Arts, a Federal Agency.

Cover design by Anita Richardson

Library of Congress Cataloguing-in-Publication Data:

Peters, Robert 1924
    Shaker Light.

    1. Lee, Ann, 1736-1784—Poetry.   I. Title.
PS3566.E756S5   1987   811'.54   86-25084
ISBN 0-87775-200-1 (alk. paper)
ISBN 0-87775-201-X (pbk. : alk. paper)

Unicorn Press, Inc.
P.O. Box 3307
Greensboro, NC 27402

The author and publisher would like to thank Anita Richardson for typesetting, in 14/14 *Deepdene*, McNaughton & Gunn for printing, on *Neutral Natural*, an acid-free sheet; Alan Brilliant, designer; Teo Savory, in-house editor; Sarah Lindsay, editorial assistant, and Leigh Carter.

for
TEO SAVORY
splendid writer, editor, publisher, friend,
and one long acquainted with the Shakers in America

LIST OF POEMS

PART THREE: THE CALL

Note, with Acknowledgements

In this book, I have followed the few outlines, so far as they are known, of Mother Ann Lee's life in America (1774-1784). My earlier work, The Gift to Be Simple (Liveright, Inc., 1975), treats the life of the Female Christ, as she was known by her followers, from her girlhood in England to her arrival in America, with eight followers, in August 1774. She was the illiterate daughter of a Manchester blacksmith. Once she had received the Call, she commanded that her followers write nothing of her for some thirty years after her death. As a result of this paucity of information, I have had to depend much upon my own intuition for rendering her elusive presence. I have on more than one occasion felt that presence as I wrote the poems. I visited numerous museums, talked with specialists in Shaker culture, and read books on the subject.

All proper names mentioned are names taken from actual Shaker history. Apart from one stanza found in the beautiful hymn, "Come, Life, Shaker Life," a portion of "One, Two, Three Step," and all of the stanzas but one of the hymn "The Humble Heart," first recorded at New Lebanon, in 1822, all songs, prayers, and hymns are of my own composing. The three winter poems, "Winter Earth-Mouths," "Ice-Storm," and "Tracks in Snow" are adaptations of a passage in Nathaniel Hawthorne's Septimus Felton. Some of the material on angels was inspired by Emanuel Swedenborg's Heaven and Hell, although the sounds angels make while singing are my own. It is noteworthy, incidentally, that a healthy number of Swedenborg's followers assembled in Manchester, England, where they were active during Ann Lee's early life there. "Herbal Remedies" is adapted from John Wesley's useful old book on folk medicine, written for his impoverished followers.

I wish to thank the Shaker sisters of Sabbathday Lake, Maine, for their hospitality and caring during my visit in August 1974 to assist in celebrating their Centennial. I shall never forget the choice experience of reading many of these poems to them, by kerosene light, in their Meeting House which still retains the original Shaker paint. Unfortunately, the three sisters living at Canterbury, blinded to Ann Lee as a living rather than a cardboard figure, withold their good will. This I regret. I wish to thank Brother Theodore Johnson, Director of Museums, Sabbathday Lake, for his generosity in sharing his wealth of information about Shaker history, and particularly for his making available to me the so-called elusive Secret Book of the Elders, an invaluable primary source of information about the early growth of the faith.

I am indebted also to Carolyn Stoloff and Paul Mariah for readings of the manuscript. E.V. Griffith's enthusiasm for these poems—some 40 of them appeared in *Poetry Now* and received a generous prize—has inspired me. I owe a particular debt to Ned Arnold who gave exceptional care to my earlier book on Mother Ann Lee. Finally, my thanks to the Corporation of Yaddo, where, in seclusion during the summer of 1975, I wrote the first versions of these poems.

Robert Peters

Huntington Beach, California
November 1985

SHAKER LIGHT

PART ONE
NEW YORK CITY

IN THE LIGHT AND DARK PLACES

A thrush's head
sliced off by a scythe
returned to its neck

A mouse
rendered limp by a cat
restored to its fleecy nest

A mower's thumb
lopped off by mistake
rejoined to its calloused hand

A cat rent and maimed
by boys
made agile and glossy again

Boys white and stiff,
like wax—drowned perhaps,
leaping the fields

    for the cat, the cat
    for the mouse, the mower
    for the thumb, the thrush
    for the grub . . .

The Lord's hints
tremble everywhere, equally
in the light and in the dark places.

ARRANGEMENTS

We go separate ways, until by signs our Heavenly Father determines the time for our gathering-in. I keep house. Abraham works in a blacksmith shop. We save whatever money we can. But money is dear. Brother James hears of a tract of wilderness, called *Niskeyuna*, near Albany. He hopes to buy the land. He believes it the site described by the blazing tree, in my vision. Abraham remains a worry. Despite our pact, he is carnal. When I remind him, he is angered and drinks. It will be better surely to take separate rooms. My presence, at night, would be a needless provocation. I shall greatly miss my friends. They weep, parting. Our tempests are presently stilled.

MOTHER ANN LEE'S FIRST VISION IN AMERICA

I see you, splendid Holy Tree
planted in Eternity.

Your tendrils strike
earth's ground, and anchor

nourishing a host of plants
all free of canker.

Your trunk drives through
the air. Deep cleaves of bark

where no scrofulous beetles lurk,
nor nibbling worms, nor moths.

Angels with golden horns
dip low, blast heavenly music

towards your trunk: *drriipppp*
drrriiipppp, toot-toot, toot-

toots of sound astound
and set the leaves a-trembling.

Oh, lavish green! Oh, leaves minute,
leaves thin, leaves flat,
leaves curled, leaves twirled!

And, oh, the angels—hummingbirds
flickering among the branches:

O Holy Tree, shed over me
Your kindly shade and beauty.

Your tremulous leaves and blossoms fair
Shake, dance, and drift as golden hair
Upon this world, that, stricken, needs Thee.
The time is near, O Holy Tree,
for Believers to be marching
With Gospel Fire and Holy Lyres,
And tabors, drums, and timbrels,
To pound and blow and trill the news
Through embouchures and with cymbals.

DICHOTOMY: ANN AND ABRAHAM

Our souls
are two broad deal boards
oiled and stained
set up to form a table.
The jointure, planed,
is well-defined.
The tincture of the grain
glistens with wax and turpentine.
Euphonious morning light.
The solid grains
make scintillations doubly bright.
At dusk, again affirming weight,
they celebrate their solid state.
The soul doth shine and glisten:

it loves its substance,
it loves its tatters,
it loves its woes, it
loves its laughter.

THE PUPPET

It's garbed in homespun, a foot high,
blue-aproned, a sash of hog-bristle,
corn husks for stuffing, pods for feet,
the neck neatly basted shut.
Sewing needles with heads broken
embedded in the lower body.
There never was a head attached.
I brush its stiff dress clean.

Pulled loose, each needle holds
a drop of honey. The doll's chest
falls and rises. I drop the creature
in the street. Its terrible laugh
is Abraham's!

THE SHAWL

I love my gray wool shawl. I found it in Mistress
Smith's attic, in a heap. "'Twas a former domestic's,"
she said. "Take it, if it fits." I find it sweet
against the wintry chill. At night it serves as an extra
comforter for the bed. I love it so, my mind divides it
into squares. Each square I name after one of my four
dead children.

TALLY

I have this day pressed and ironed

    8 large bed sheets
    9 dresses, 6 of them pleated, with lace
    8 handkerchiefs
    3 waistcoats of green cotton bound with tape
    1 mantle ("mandilion") lined with cotton
    4 night shirts
10 handtowels
12 serviettes
    6 large linen tablecloths

In addition,

    I have scrubbed

        the entire entranceway with soda
        the stairs, including all rungs
        the ordure-boxes in the five bedrooms
        all the surfaces in both laundry and kitchen.

And yet, Mistress complains that I am tardy in my tasks!

HUMBLE TASKS: I

To slam a door in pique,
or a firkin, is
a screaming. To drop
a pan in haste
is to slice a knife
through your life.
Go gracefully
about your house, move
like a heavenly dancer.
Sweep, mop, scour the room
up to the rafters!

SUNDAY

We walk to the wharves. Whiffs of cloud.
Sparkling day. *The Mariah* rides at anchor
where she docked a fortnight ago. She is
becalmed. Her masts where the angel rode
are blackened fire. I find it hard to see
the plank beaten loose by the water,
the plank that saved us when the captain
threatened to throw us overboard for
worshipping on deck. Yes, there it is!
The rime on the decks! A flash of sun!
A sign reads: *This Shippe for Biddes as Salvage.*

THE INDIAN

He is quite sinewy and tall.
I have no fear of him at all
and sit some distance on,
where from the shade I can observe his motions.
He seems at peace, his red brows creased,
his stalwart arms at rest,
folded over his chest.
I wonder if his gods are true,
and what receiving the gospel would do.
Ignorant of the tongue he speaks
I waft His love, a divine afflatus
from above, to touch his Soul.
The forests are rampant with his race.
God, work wonders on that stalwart face!

MILITIA

Men drilling on the green. Real muskets
and real powder. We keep our distance,
since a day ago a coxcomb broke the ranks
and berated Abraham: "George the Third
don't keep his word. Those who won't drill
are traitors. Grab a musket, chicken gizzard!
You're an English spy!"
Jeering from the marching men.

A PLAIN SONG

Wigs and perukes
are fine for dukes
and princes of the realm,
and beauty-marks upon the cheeks
of duchesses suit them well.

But as for me
I'll draw my hair into a handsome knot
and keep my face as clear as rain
and free of social blots.

KING GEORGE AT DINNER

King George eats partridge
lamb and venison.
He belches wine and farts.
The waiters replenish cakes and tarts.

George shouts German expletives
deplores the Bostonians
routs the Colonials
with orotund imperatives.

Fearing an apoplectic bout,
the servants struggle,
carry him out.

FOUR VIGNETTES OF SPRING

1.

The Hudson is a gray coat:
tributaries are its sleeves.
Four bodies float therein,
men wearing the uniform of the king.

2.

Rain driven at obtuse angles.
A dozen crows dangle
from evergreen boughs.
A fair dinner.

3.

An Iroquois inspects my blister.
He departs, returns with sumac leaves.
He chews the leaves and smears the blister.
It bursts: the leaves, like columbine,
are a splendid anodyne.

4.

Pussywillows and catkins.
Oakbuds and daffodils.
The robins are here.
The meadowlarks are coming.
Pussywillows and catkins.
Oakbuds and daffodils.

REVOLUTION

Mistress tells of Boston men dumping English tea
into the harbor. There's talk of dumping other goods
as well. The Colonials are for war, Mistress says,
for *Revolution*. The king's insane and is perdition.
The antidote, she claims, though risky, is sedition.
Abraham should join the cause. No, I explain, we strive
to keep our spirits free, savoring Heaven's liberty.

Larks and fishes sweep my brain's heart and proscenium.
The dirt of Manchester falls. Larks of the English sky,
the dace and bream of English streams
dissolve in visions. I tamp down Colonial sod,
am one with God.

SKYSCAPE

A wedge of silver
ripped open, then covered.
An orb, yea,
but at once a seal
round and milky.
Indigo clouds
flow over the harbor.
The sun eats
its own edge now,
ever to live!

CHOLERA

Rumor says that a ship of English troops,
landing in Boston, brings cholera.
Some of the crew are dead,
a number linger with horribly swollen limbs
and bellies. The air is noisome today!

THE FIRE

A mute scuffling on the cobblestones.
Dusk. Rosy smoke
within a dozen rods of here.
A house on fire.

If we are to burn, if
we are to turn, Abraham, husband,
in our dwelling, in our damp house,
its quail-body shingles loosening,
niter on each shingle,
foot-places hollowed in each stair . . .
husband, where are you? You left
to buy bread and cheese.

I wait in this burning street.
Are you drinking ale?
I turn, but see no one.
The burned house sinks in its ashes.
The sun is down too.
My spirit falls like an old shoe.
Husband, what shall we do?

HUNGER

A kindly woman gives us pease-pudding, pickled eggs
and ginger conserve. For we are now both turned
from our employment. Mistress Smith contracts another
housekeeper, saying she cannot wait until my husband is
mended. Master Smith refuses to rehire Abraham,
on any account, saying he is "unreliable, given over as he is
to sundry whorings." We are reduced to cadging leaves
from vegetable stalls.

ABRAHAM'S GIFT

A linnet in a fiber cage
swinging from a ceiling,
a greenish bird, wondrous,
to woo me night and morning.

His trills of sound outfly my doubt
that Abraham's gift is truly
meant to show me that without
sexual love I really

warp my soul and cause his ache
to daily grow injurious.
I change the linnet's marvellous song
to hymns of Heaven's making

and trill them with full-throated joy,
my physical burn abating.

CLOSURE

1.

O, this bird casts my breath on the air.
My chest's hollow.

2.

I see a fiber cage.
A minuscule black hand, all fingers
folded, the index finger pointing,
crushes the bird's throat.

3.

I'd have preferred an ivory bird,
a giftless songster, speeding
to this house, to its shallows,
to its depths below the stairs,
to its chimneys and sculleries,
to its awful closures.

THE LESSON

Force a reed up a frog.
Blow, reversing the pressure,
exploding its brain.
Cast the frog into a pool.
Splayed, he floats,
a giddy expression on his face.
"Look," you say, "it's better than arsenic."

BREASTS

The hard gums of my dead children
bite for milk. Elisabeth
suckles the longest.
Perhaps that's why she lived.
John gives up the breast
three weeks after birth, and dies.
The other two die before they set any pattern.

My breast's brown nipple-aureole
is near my face. I smell
fecund milk-syrup.
The nipple stands erect.
Its mouth is open.
I bring my lips an inch away,
but can't touch to suck it.

If I nourish the world
who will nourish me?
Sweet milk. Sweet milk of Heaven,
drench me!

VISIT FROM ELISABETH

1.

In a large wheat ear
wrapped in mist—an
effulgent child appears.

An adamantine protecting husk,
a scarlet seat
in the center of the wheat.

An image, as of a narthex
or a nave. The wheat drifts
higher, to my table

where I slake my hunger
by drinking vinegar
and rolling my tongue under.

2.

The child steps out upon the table.
In the shimmer
I do not see the face.

"Mother, I am Elisabeth
your daughter come from Heaven
to visit you."

3.

I place my hand, palm up,
fingers opened, near her.
Elisabeth! It is indeed no other!

Lightly, bare-footed,
she steps into my hand.
The hem of her white gown.

She kisses my lips.
"Peace, peace," she exclaims.
"Satan is screaming in his flames.

"Be as a child, Mother dear.
Nor fear the carnal. God's eye
is on you, ever near.
Sweet is the balm of Gilead."

4.

Air weights the room.
I think I will be crushed.
Air flings me toward the ceiling,
spins me around, then sets me down
unhurt upon the floor. My child
is gone. The weeds I'd picked
are also gone: plantain, dandelion
and thistle. And in their place
these spirit-gifts arrayed along a cross:

    a loaf of bread sliced and
    spread with butter, a basket
    of white roses, spectacles
    for seeing Truth distinctly,
    a scarlet robe the length
    of a finger embalmed
    with myrrh and aloes,
    small spiced cakes of Love,
    two flames of Gospel Fire,
    a tiny broom for sweeping out
    dark corners of the heart,
    celestial wine in thimble goblets,
    a silver chain fastened
    by the Clasp of Obedience . . .

My heart sweetens in meditation.

THE BIRD FREED

There's a whiff of air.
A feather settles.

The room drifts with juicy spiders
to be eaten.

Come, linnet, fly, fly,
sweet linnet, fly.

THE ANGEL

I see an angel on a field
skimming o'er the snow.
He never once does tumble.

But suddenly
in a shower of flame
he veers, spins, and crumples.

I seek to give him courage
a balsam for his pain.
I brush the ice from off his wings
and set him aloft again.

THE SNAKE

I kiss his slack throat.
Buds of wheat ears go on swelling.
Ants race among the plants
stripped of leaves, near my heels.

Blood gushing from his throat is cold.
Blood gushing from my mouth is warm.
He means no harm.

CHRISTMAS EVE

1.

I promise Abraham he can stay the night.
"For the babes," he says. Two
(both males) were conceived on
Christmas Eve. He still suffers
for their deaths, cannot accept, nor will,
(yea) that they are in Heaven.
"They stroke my face," he says.
"Elisabeth is crying. I hear her every night."

2.

He brings mistletoe. "I found it
in the street, a sprig dropped
by a wassailer." He embraces me.
His breath is sweet, no hint
of gin. With care we sit
beside the hearth. He rubs my knees.
"Lass, you're pretty," he says.
I'm wearing a fresh blue smock,
his favorite color. I stroke
the hairs on his hands. I want
to kiss his forehead—
not a wrinkle there, not a scar.
"We should live together, lass," he says.
"Would you like some cider?"
"I would," he says. I bring the glass.
He pulls me to his lap.
Slabs of ice slide from the roof.
The house creaks and settles.

3.

In bed, in our warm nightshifts
there's a sword between us.
Beyond this we must not roll,
nor must I move.
"Please, lass, let me stroke your hair.
There's no harm surely."
My skin glows where he touches it.
A needle burns my hand.
The burn strikes my brain. He turns,
kissing my hair.
The moan I make cannot be mine.
His hand (I help him) probes my groin.
He thrusts his fingers.
A flood of wet! The wet is my bleeding!

NEW YEAR'S DAY, 1775

Snowcrust. An ice-storm, horrendous,
of a sort I never saw in England.
Even the chickadees, dismayed,
plant themselves on window sills
and wait. Dogs slip and grovel
in the street. Spring's cocoons
ensconced in furry ice.

And here we stand.
Five months nearer Zion, the Promised Land.
Brother James and Mary Partington are well.
The Hocknells, no doubt, will arive from England
in the spring. We live dutiful lives:
my chores exhaust me. Few hours left for prayer.

EVICTION

The landlord demands that I quit his premises.
"I'll stay a fortnight," I declare. "I have
already paid. I will not leave before then."
"As of today, the furniture's extra, ma'am.
Four shillings, ha'penny."

I cannot pay the extra sum,
so I am dispossessed of my tiny room.

CHILL AND COLD

I lie on the floor, under a shawl.
The boards, *listen*, snap with ice.
Slice my distress, Lord. Bleed me.
Release phlegm, release fire!

ABRAHAM'S VISIT

"I've come to see thee, Ann,
to see how you be faring."

"You may come in. Please,
shut the door behind thee."

"Here is some money. There's not much.
It's a swift life I'm leading."

"Who waits behind thee in the hall?
I see a person in a shawl."

"Her name's Sweet Charity.
Come forward, Miss. This is my Ann . . ."

"Greetin's, I'm sure. Abe tells me
you're inspired by The Word, a livin' Bible."

"Who is this person, pray?
I do not want her here, tho' her name be Charity.

"Look, Miss, do not parade thyself about,
as if to do a fandango. This is the Devil's whoring."

"Ann, we've seen the roughest parts of life,
and if we can't be man and wife
I won't be here tomorrow."

IN A STRANGE TONGUE: A TALISMAN FOR ILLNESS

Langia swithin in wornamin
Swith ofra, swith nefra
Wornamin pentangela, luss
Wornamin, wornamin, sen-sun

Spare Abraham!

Rantidon, tindown, lip
spittle, chockaloo.
Langia swithin in wornamin.
Death's langia swithin, langia
Swithin in wornamin.

Spare Abraham!

THE DEAD

The dead lying on a vast bed
of jonquils and chrysanthemums—
all the dead, I mean, who've ever lived.

The living (all the living, I mean) stand
on a coign of land, their backs to a meadow.

ILLNESS

I prepare salted haberdyne for Abraham. Perhaps,
since I've soaked the salt from the cod, he can
swallow it, with broth and a wash of vinegar.
I shall stay by him through the delirium. Yesterday
his fever seemed lifted. But, today it returns
doubly vengeful. I keep soaked cloths on his head.
I wipe his chest with hot vinegar. The haberdyne
is cooked, so I place it on a dish, in flakes.

I must doze, even if only for seconds, in this hard
chair. I cannot leave Abraham to return to my room.
He is on his back. Guttural noises choke his throat.
Seamy with dried spittle, his mouth hangs open. His
eyes are shut. I cannot wake him. I kneel and pray.
A black bear claws my skull. I count his hairs.
I count his breaths. He is eating me.

AZRAEL

Azrael, angel of death
spins swiftly
round my husband's head
where he is dying in his bed.

Azrael licks an empty gruel bowl.
He eats fish.
He eats wax. He wails.
Roaches cling to the creases
in his face. Beetles chomp matter
from his eyes. He tries
a one-claw footing on a chair.
He tears his hair and screams.

I beat the angel with a broom.
Abraham is up, standing by the window.

THE WHELKS OF DEATH

The open window releases stench, the rancid
butter scraped from death's cadaver: the whelks
of death. I burn the bedding. Sick-worms
sizzle and squirm. Tonight we sleep
beneath fresh sheets. Between us on the floor,
bread and cheese, a candle, and a flask of water.
We shall never be frightened again
by the whelks, by the whorled ears of death.

PART TWO:
NISKEYUNA—ANGELS OF ABUNDANCE

CLOUDS

The sun behind a cloud,
five swallows wing easily north,
a breeze ruffles a grove of sumacs.
Whispers, yes, a splendid witnessing!

The clouds froth:
one is England, Scotland, Wales.
Another is the neck of a mother.
Little spears topmost on the spruce
rise: arboreal exclamation marks of God!

CHOSEN HOME

Sumac must be hewn down,
and larch, maple, and birch,
nettles, pine and grape vine—
before we can plant
potatoes, squash, and maize.
And, as the season's early,
we hope to grow considerable barley.

DRESS

My brown dress is of homespun.
My kerchief is of muslin.
My bonnet is of pasteboard
covered with cotton.

My shoes are handsewn leather
with uppers of linen.
My shawl, though threadbare,
is worsted woolen.

Someday in Jerusalem
we shall all be wearing
white robes of linen
and kerchiefs of soft cambric.

WILLIAM LEE DREDGES A SWAMP

William Lee has a dredge for clearing swamps:
a rough plank six feet long and three feet broad, hewn
from a pine, with projecting boards fastened at right
angles with braces. William places boulders, one on
each end of the dredge, attaches the whole to horses,
wades the horses into the marsh, drives the dredge against
the marsh islands and tumbles them over. Soon he has
fashioned a pond, which the dredge deepens. The loam is
peat-like. The bank will be luxurious. The pond will
supply irrigation, and, stocked with fish, will furnish
much food. Waterfowl will nest here, and, in droughts
(since it is spring fed) it will supply drinking water.
Next, the men intend to locate spring freshets further out,
dredge and channel them in to the pond, so that, in time,
the water will drive a wheel, the wheel will drive a mill,
the mill will drive our husbandry.

FOOD GATHERING

Hazel, hickory, and walnuts, we lay by a-plenty.
Twenty bushels of wild rice, from the Iroquois. Six
tons of marsh hay for our livestock. Pecks of potatoes,
bushels of barley, red apples, currants and gooseberries,
crooknecked squash, pumpkins, carrots buried in the sand
of our common larder house.

We count each thing exactly, towards the stark winter.
James Whittaker, who is in charge, will ration the food
precisely. We must be frugal. These are not yet days
of plenty.

THE ANT

A pismire
  lugs his grainy egg
over the sand
  to a crevice in a stone,
his home.

A wolf
  nearly crushes him
but through a space
  between those hairy toes
the ant escapes.

In a flood, the ant floats
  wide upon the tide
secures himself a ride
  on a drifting log
and sails along.

God's plan is clear:
  the meek and the infinitesimal
inherit the earth!

HUMBLE TASKS: II

Humble tasks patten to the ground.
God savors every one.

Along the stars, God's milk.

My head fades back.
I gasp choking on the Heaven-sent thick stream!

AS THE **BIRD** WINGS IN TO THE TREE

The hesitancy of a bird
approaching a tree
resembles our winging in
to Eternity:
    as we near that place
of celestial green
with prospects, lawns and willowy sheen,
we soar up
towards the nearest limb,
slowing our flight,
with our claws stretched right,
avid to enter the Kingdom
to worship Him.

A CONUNDRUM

A bloated trout
is jostled by marsh weeds.
Flies collect
upon his side and linger
at his fundament.
I wish a turtle
would pull him under:
he's such an emblem,
a conundrum.

RUGS AND MOCCASINS

1.

For your earthen floor
gather cattail reeds
of a substantial length,
and interweave them
so that the yanking to-
gether is tight.
Sew a binding to all edges.
If firmly knit
your reed mat
will keep out some,
albeit not all,
the frost this winter.

2.

For moccasins (the Iroquois
taught me this) take
choice cornhusks interwoven,
and fashion them to the feet.
Similarly, suit the upper part
snug to the ankle.
These shoes are fine for summer,
spring and fall. In winter
they are comfortable
only near the hearth.

ANGELS AT THEIR BAKING

Ko-num, ko-num
sing the angels
at their simple tasks
so cheery. One punches
bread *(ko-num, ko-num-num)*.
One peels apples in single parings
(ko-num dee-lee).

Another whirrs his wings
and makes a hasty pudding
(ko-num, ko-num).
Another concocts a tasty partridge pie
(ko-num, ko-num).

Oh, celestial angels baking,
your sweet concoctions making,
bless us as we too
our routine chores perform.

Each whisk of our spoons,
each beat of our ladles,
each push of our wrists
into dough, meat, or whey
praises our Father
(the sweetest confection)
who guides our spirits
through this joyous day.

Ko-num, ko-num, e, o,
vira, vir-de-lay.

STRAWBERRIES AND MOSQUITOES

Wild strawberries are so numerous,
succulent, and plump
we fill our baskets in an hour.

The mosquitoes are as large
as wasps. The welts, if scratched,
swell to the size of wren's eggs.

SMOKING

I love the long clay pipe
James Whittaker made for me.
Smoking it's so peaceful.
It gently drifts my cares away
and makes my soul more tuneful.

Praise, Heavenly Father,
for this gift, and thanks be
to the Indians, who taught us
how to puff this weed
and thereby blessed your minions.

FERNS

Ferns coiled like springs, or bishop's
croziers. Most carry fern-wool, used
by birds for lining nests.
"Circinate vernation," this
unique uncoiling of the ferns.

Plucked when their wool is fresh,
and boiled lightly, garnished with onion,
they are delicious and are indispensable,
since they fight inflammations
of the intestines and catarrhs.

HERBAL REMEDIES

Comfrey roots boiled to a thick mucilage, as a poultice,
relieves *Sprained Tendons*.

A carrot poultice nearly cold, or agrimony leaves
pounded, relieves *Putrid Wounds and Gangrene*.

Powdered fern-root boiled and bear's leaves sprinkled
with vinegar, stamped and strained, relieve *Flat and Round
Worms*.

For the *Whites*, live chastely, exercise constantly
and never sleep on your back. Also, boil 4 or 5 hollyhock
(white) petals in a pint of milk.

Juice of marigold flowers, or bruised purslain, or daily
rubbing with a radish relieves *Warts*.

A decoction of yarrow relieves *Bloody Urine*.

To stop *Vomiting*, slit a large onion across the grain
and apply it to the pit of the stomach.

Decoctions of mint followed with a sprinkle of
finely powdered rue, or ashes from the gross stalks
on which red coleworts grow, or poultices of boiled
parsnips relieve *Malignant Ulcers*.

For *Viper Bite* apply bruised garlic. To prevent
snakebite, rub hands in radish juice.

Bean flowers boiled in 3 parts of water and 1 of vinegar
relieve *Inflamed Testicles*.

72

To cure *Toothache*, rub roasted turnip parings hot
behind the ear, or put a leaf of betony up the nose,
or lay boiled nettles to the cheek, or hold a slice of apple
lightly boiled between the teeth. The ashes of burned
bread are excellent for *Cleaning the Teeth*.

For *Wasp Stings*, rub the stung part with the bruised
leaves of house-leek, watercress, or rue.

For *Skin Rubbed Off*, apply pounded heal-all, or a bit
of white paper with spittle.

For *Pleurisy*, core an apple, fill it up with white
frankincense, stop it close with the piece you cut out,
roast it in ashes, mash and eat it.

To prevent *The Plague*, eat marigold flowers, daily, as
a salad, with oil and vinegar, or, infuse rue, sage,
mint, rosemary, wormwood, of each a handful, into two
quarts of the sharpest vinegar, over warm embers
for 8 days—strain it through a funnel and add half an
ounce of camphor, and with this wash the loins, face, and
mouth, and snuff a little up the nose when you go abroad
where there may be infectious persons.

A bruised onion skinned, or roasted in ashes, perfectly cures
Dry Piles.

For relieving *Lunacy*, shave the head, anoint it with
ivy-leaves infused with vinegar, and chafe the head
every other day for three weeks. This also generally cures
Melancholy.

For *Falling of the Fundament* apply a cloth covered thick with
brick-dust, or apply a handful of boiled red rose leaves as hot
as can be borne.

For *Consumption*, try two handsful of sorrel in a pint of whey
boiled and strained, or a cow heel ready dressed with
2 quarts of milk, 2 ounces of hartshorn shavings, 2 ounces
of isinglass, a quarter pound of sugar candy, and a trace of
ginger. Put all these in a pot in an oven after the bread
is drawn. Let the consumptive live on this concoction. In the
last stage of the disease suck a healthy woman daily.

MOTHER ANN CHOPS WOOD IN A FOREST

Towers of pitch-pine forests
form whited coverts for hares.
Stubborn red oaks keep their leaves,
whipping the winds.
An icy freshet smashes a dam.
On a fence of upturned roots
a flock of snow buntings:
a wheeling flight amid feathery snow weeds.
My shadow is Elysian.
From my bonnet to my husk-wrapped
boots, I am blue-shadow Persian.
I am enraptured with my own wood-
chopping shadow, my amethyst hatchet.

THE WOOD-RICK

"Brother James, your rick of split white birch
looks quite solid and symmetrical."

"Mother, when snowstorms buffet
it may tumble and be lost till spring."

"Do, pray, let it stand. The season's brief,
and there is harvesting to do."

"I can't allow it, Mother. To right it
is to align it with God.
I want this rick even and good."

STAPLES

Rice is needed,
as is flour, and tubs
of lard, salt, and molasses.
Two hours of sun
before the snow resumes.
Drifts must be
ten feet deep by now.
It takes an hour
to thrash to the barn
where the cows bray
over their scant allotment of hay.
As for myself, apart from some tea
made of spruce bark and wintergreen,
I've had nothing to eat today.

WINTER EARTH-MOUTHS

Fog invests our vales.
All creatures, exhaling,
create frost-work—
the earth's breath made visible.
The mightiest trees
are palinodes of sparkling.
Walking beneath them in the fog
we see as the ant sees,
or as the leaping snow-flea.
The rigid trees are soft,
spirits without a marked edge
or outline.
A flock of snow geese wings over
honking.

ICE-STORM

Here is an aster (savory-leaved)
    its flat, imbricated
        calyxes, three-quarters

of an inch broad
    are encased in a translucent
        ice-button

a glass knob
    beneath which shimmers
        a brown calyx.

The blue-curl calyx
    has a spherical button
        like those on a boy's jacket

and the pennyroyal
    smaller still, has ice
        spheres about its stem

arranged
    chandelier-wise
        and still fragrant

through the ice.
    Fine marsh-grass supports
        wonderful burdens

of ice: bent over into
    countless incredible little arches,
        with each step you take
they crash and crumble.

TRACKS IN SNOW

1.

Mouse tracks on the pure snow
  unbroken by bushes or grasses
five rods across, three wide,
  tracks running from the bushes on one side
to those on the other
  the tracks quite near together,
repeatedly crossing each other
  at acute angles, the tail marks
joining the four paw marks in the powder.

2.

Mouse bodies seem airy
  to have muffled their snow
paths with leaping, hieing
  to see neighbors on the other side
of the meadow, in the hazel-brush thicket.
  Our souls, like deermice
without guile or contumely, cross and criss-cross
  the soft snows with tracks of delight.

WOUNDS

Wounded,
we do not seal away
the clubs, whips, razors
and glass, the fangs
in the wilderness.

Faith
is Christ's blood
imbibing itself.
Snowfields of joy:
cornfields resound
with hearts alive
drained of bile:

    Nothing we do is purposeless.
    Cycles of time spin
    over the dead clocks,
    the stifled hearts of victims.

After they've healed,
all wounds
remember their perpetrators.

81

IMPRISONED IN POUGHKEEPSIE

1.

Imprisoned in Albany
and moved to Poughkeepsie
when my gaolers believe
I am an English spy.
Through the bars of my cell
I convert numerous persons
who have gathered in this yard
to hear good gospel news.
Yesterday two hundred
came to my preaching.

2.

My gaolers do not beat me
although at times they shove me
and withhold my food saying
"That, my dear, will tame you."

My singing, joy and laughter
shame two turnkeys
who become disciples
and thereby lose their jobs.

Now they'll labor for me
in the forests of Niskeyuna,
for the furtherance of the Word
in a communal livelihood.

3.

Come then, O gaolers, take me
to new keepers. You may
transport my body, you
cannot quench my witness
or stifle my caroling.
And the faithful shall follow me
from Albany to Poughkeepsie
or to any spot you deign
to set me free again.
Come, then, gaolers,
why do you tarry?
Shackle my wrists and arms
and hurry me to the English.

GAOL

I place a chair on a table,
climb upon the chair.
Blood, Sweat, Prison-Stones.

I kneel for hours praying without moving.
An angel sweetens my tongue.
He wipes my brow with his hair.

I see stunted olive trees,
wild ground-ivy,
boulders, thorns, jasmine.

And the sweet stars caroling!
The sweat of these mossy stones *is*
the blood-sweat of Jesus.

NO SPECK OF BLOOD IS TOO
MINUSCULE FOR GOD TO LOVE

A gnat strikes.
I smash him. His black speck
bubbles and runs like pudding
down my hand.

God takes each aster
as his own, each rose.
He sets each blood-flame
near his throne.

THE HANGED MAN

The hanged man frantic
    wishes to be crucified upside down.
But, his executioners burn out his tongue
    and let him hang upright
until the worms eat him down.

Two bread-rolls and a slab of cheese
    will put any executioner at his ease.
And, if he's a man of faith
    add poison and watch him breathe.

SATAN, VISITOR

Satan flies in
with his implacable hands out
and sits by my fire.

"There's no dirt in heaven," I say,
taking a broom and tidying the room
near His Majesty.

Cobwebs drift over his feet,
charred ashes and lime smear his hooves.
He takes the blown dust
up his nose like snuff.

ANGEL VISITORS

Six angels in samite
wearing rubies and carbuncles
hover over the field in a row.
I am tilling peas and beans.

One angel whips the air with his wings:

> "Those who believe in a Trinity
> may not be admitted to Eternity:
> for Sophistry
> roils the mind, as does a jiggling
> of terms. Such people feed the worms."

A second angel speaks:

> "Ann, children are the elect of Heaven.
> At their transubstantiation
> they wax in wisdom
> until eventually, sooner
> than adults foresee, they
> achieve the essences of angels,
> of a primal necessity."

I am dancing! My feet are off the ground!

A third angel, taller than the rest
and more regal, chants:

> "Ann, the interior mind, yours,
> is arrayed, like an angel's mind,
> in the Form of Heaven. Heaven is
> the Human Form Divine."

A fourth angel strikes his forehead:

"Wicked souls who by mischance reach Heaven
writhe, gasp, and leap about like fishes
out of water, or like animals
in ether, in an air-pump when
the air's exhausted. Ann, be an angel,
a Heaven. Be the female Christ!"

A fifth angel produces an almanac
scribbled on a white board trimmed in gold.
The board speaks:

"The head is intelligence and wisdom
The breast is charity
The loins are marriage-loves
The arms and hands are truths unfolding
The feet mark what is natural
And where you must go physically
The eyes are the understanding
The nostrils are perception
The ears are obedience
And the kidneys the scrutiny of Truth.

The Greatest Man is Heaven.
Heaven is the Greatest Form
    of the Greatest Man."

The final angel shakes his wings:

"Watch for us, watch for us from the East, especially
as a society, during fatigue, in the fields, at the mill,
at home. Watch for a cloud glowing white and turning red.

The cloud will seem a perfect human form. Watch for stars
about the cloud. These are the angels, the cloud is Heaven.
All angels face the Lord, and turn with Him as he turns the
Cosmos. Men turn their faces. They mark the light with
praise, the dark with lanterns. Turn toward and away from
the rain, turn into and against the gale. How else, Mother,
to explain sorrow?''

The angels, grouped, sing a hymn, ecstatic, scraps of phrases and
words from the holy psalms:

Chanta, chanta, chantizes
chasta, chasta, chastizes

He slays them, lewd, shews them,
shrewd, his angels: thyself, thee,
th, th, th, th, th, th, thy,
plant an ear on a tree, plant
an ear of grain, who shall hear?
Plant an eye, as Satan goes by.

> *tin-sin, tin, sin, tin-tin-sin*
> give his angels, ancient his angels,
> *say-tin.*

Exalt his horn, anoint his fat, his throne.

Below and old. Be bold and old.
Be below and old. O Lord, my foot
slippeth, my foot slippeth badly.
Thy mercy holds me. Now, my soul
slippeth not, nor slippeth my joy.
Thy mercy! Thy mercy!

NIGHTMARE

What is it? A shuffling beast with its legs
in a coat of hair. And here are hands, pelfed,
fur-swatched, yea. I can't get free!
My fingers are strips clinging to knucklebone.
Gaolers, I have been imprisoned too long.
I want to go home.

RELEASE

Governor Clinton releases me
from the prison in Poughkeepsie,
and sets free David Darrow, John
Hocknell, and Joseph Meacham
from the city jail at Albany.

MOTHER IS HOME!

1.

The beak cracks the shell.
The body, yolky, sequined with shell-scraps
falls forth.

2.

We bleat our love in God's pastures.
How simply we graze, how safe from wolves.
Our faith's our fleece. Mother's spirit graces
our lips—a butterfly on roses.

"LABORING"

We mortify via laboring, that is
we sanctify our beings by bowing,
shaking, rolling, screaming in tongues,
bending and twirling.

We hop on one leg about the dwelling,
trembling, groaning, swinging our arms.

Then, of a sudden, we break off for
smoking and joking and frequent fits
of laughter (brothers and sisters
equally partaking).

Thus we rinse our spirits clean.
Thus, laboring, we spin our lives
into filaments of silver.
Praise the Lord! Mother is home!

92

SMALL FISHES ARE MOVING

1.

Pike-weed and waterfern
stroke the fish and hide them
from the jaws of turtles
and giant grass-pickerel.

Small fish are flashing
in the streams of Heaven.
Waterweeds glow
with affinity and love.

2.

They are coming, my children! My visions reveal
the miraculous burgeoning of our splendid faith.
They shall flock hither as doves, as numerous
as sandgrains—so, my loved ones, lay up stores
for their coming. Prepare dances, spinnings and
swirlings, swirlings and turnings.

PART THREE
THE CALL

THE CALL

O hearken, believers,
the time is auspicious
for following the urgings
of numerous visitations
and going on pilgrimage
throughout New England.

A Faith cannot strengthen
nor God's wisdom grow
unless they're annealed
in rain, sleet, and snow.

PENTECOSTALS AND OTHERS ARRIVE AT NISKEYUNA TO BE GATHERED-IN (1780-1781)

1.

David Meacham came from Enfield
    to sit at Mother's hearth.
He was a man of wealth and honor.
    Mother felt he would be a great preacher
but his father opposed his faith.
    With the help of God and Mother
David converted his father.
    Both were devoted Shakers until their dying day.

2.

Samuel Johnson was a preacher
    of the Presbyterian faith. From Yale,
he gave prestige to Mother's work,
    was joined by *Daniel Goodrich*,
son of a deacon in the Baptist church.

3.

John Farrington was a young man
    with boils upon his back,
with proof of Mother's wisdom
    as she described the sins
he'd been reluctant to confess.
    "I know all the things you've ever done,
John Farrington, and more.
    They flashed upon my inner mind
as you stepped through the door."

4.

Ebenezer Cooley saw our Mother in a vision
    before he took the faith.
She was the spiritual copy of the woman at Niskeyuna:
    short, thickset, light, and fair.
Her eyes were keen and blue.
    When he knelt to kiss her seemly skirt
she said, "Friend, that will do.
    Please rise and save your rapture,
for your faith will be tested,
    and your person will be whipped and beaten
for following our Gospel Way."

5.

John Denny, without a penny, came to Mother:
    his child had swallowed a button
no physician could remove.
    As John Denny's child was dying,
Mother blessed John Denny crying.
    "Go home," she said, "and *see*.
Then find yourself employment."

    His son was in his cradle
playing with the button, and on the table
    was a joint of steaming mutton.

6.

Hezekiah Hammond, a young consumptive,
    came as a scoffer. He swung
a fancy horsewhip while Father William
    preached the Gospel.
William turned upon Hezekiah:
    "You idle man, and irreverent,
put down that whip at once.
    Your lungs are charred with arrogance,
your brain is a feverish mush."
    God's Power struck the young doubter
and pinioned his arms as if for an execution.

Hammond's consumption faded.
    His lungs blew fresh clean air.
God's Love was in him, as he began madly dancing there.

7.

Zadock Wright, a Royalist, lost his lands
    at Canterbury, was imprisoned at Albany,
heard and believed Mother's prophecy
    that the Colonials would beat the English.
He saw the warming blaze of Mother's heavenly
    lantern, and entered the portals of Heaven
as a staunch Believer newborn.

8.

John Cotton, a New-Lighter, visited *James Jewett*,
        a Shaker. After breakfast one morning
whilst the two men were talking
        John was raised from his chair
and spun "swiftly round," in a rush of sound
        for the space of an hour.
Out of the door he flew, still in sitting position,
        over the stones and the stumps
to the shores of Lake Mascoma.
        Here he hovered, absorbing the view
till the spirit whirled him anew
        and spun him back to the kitchen,
to the same brown chair he had sat in.
        This event, he declared, "sealed" his faith.
He gave up any further journey
        and settled in Connecticut.

9.

Then appeared *Esther Bracket*, *Thankful Barce*,
        and *Mary Knapp* whose daughter
reviled Mother as "an horrible drunken squaw,
        an Indian lover."
She shook her curls and said
        she'd never join that "crazy woman's Shakers."
Within a week *Miss Hannah Knapp*
        endured a terrible miscarriage—
the unblessed fetus was foul with hair
        and had a loathsome twisted appendage!
Mary Knapp slapped her daughter
        and admonished her to be reverent.
Mother Ann received the girl, and treating her
        most kindly, looked up to see the Spirit of God
as a snow-white dove flying.

101

TURNING SONG

Whatever is taken returns.
Whatever is lost is found.
Turn, turn, Believer, turn right round.

The sky again is blue.
The trapped hare is sprung.
Turn, turn, Believer, turn right round.

Whatever dies quickens.
Whatever is tied is unbound.
Turn, turn, Believer, turn right round.

Whatever is eyeless, sees.
Whatever is dumb cries angel-sounds.
Turn, Believer, turn right round.

JOURNEYING

Snowdrops cluster at our feet.
  We have traveled thirty miles today.
We eat waterlily roots, raw eggs and bread for supper.
  The horses pasture in a glade.
Father sends radiant doves to guide us.
  We push five more miles, together, until dusk.

SATAN

In pursuit of his tail
mistaking it for a jonquil
Satan races two hundred miles.
He is last observed heading north,
which should put him
nearly out of the country,
well in the vicinity
of the St. Lawrence River.

BASS

A school of bass, all together,
two dozen, each a foot long.
Their green tails flicker.
Five of them we catch for dinner.

SOUVENIRS OF MOVING

The hull of the black carriage
drawn by the horse with the great withers
who never tarries
as the wheels rattle
riding to Massachusetts.
Who is better carried than I,
by the horse with the great withers?

THE JOURNEY: I

We visit Tucconock Mountain, sixty miles from Albany.
We reach Enfield, and meet our first hostility:
threats from the townfolk directed towards David Meacham.
Then on to Grafton, from thence to Still River
to see Zaccheus Stevens. A pleasant stop
with Isaac Willard at Harvard. Then to Littleton and
Shirley, both in the vicinity, where rumors abound
that we are English spies, producing in secret
seventy wagons of supplies and six hundred stands of weapons.

A SOUL WHOSE FAITH BURNS HOT

I am Richard Treat.
I wander through a storm to Mother's fire.
She bids me dry my clothes and feeds me.
James Whittaker washes my feet.

"Richard Treat," exclaims an Elder,
standing by the fire.
"Thou hast neither cold nor heat,
are lukewarm in thy faith.
I spew thee into the fire!"

I strike my skull upon the floor
and lie for an hour before sensing Mother's power.

"Richard Treat's a man who prays.
He's ready for confession. Come, Elder William,
take this man to absolution."

I am a Believer eternally,
a Soul whose faith burns hot, hot,
a Soul whose faith burns hot.

THE JOURNEY: II

We carry our mission to Petersham,
to Thomas Shattuck's.
At Meeting, on a Sabbath,
the enemy snuff out the lights.

Elisabeth Shattuck fights so fiercely
that Mother flees her captors.
Some thirty men break down the doors.
They beat David Hammond.
His wife, clutching her child,
tries to assist him and is beaten.

The ruffians find Mother
crouched in a closet. They pummel
and revile her. They drag her,
feet foremost, to a waiting sleigh.
Men taunt her with obscenities.
Her dress and cap are ruined.
To see if she be God
they expose her private parts.

Beating their horses, they start
their wretched journey. But, using
our bodies, we keep the sleigh from moving.

Ann is brought to Samuel Peckham
who commands that she be stripped
for the prurience of her captors.
Brave David Hammond leaps on a table
and harangues so persuasively
that Peckham is dissuaded

from his loathsome business.
Filled with remorse now
he promises the Shakers
they may go in peace.

Back at Thomas Shattuck's
Mother enters singing
in the sweetest voice
that ever mortals heard.
The Lord has delivered her,
the Lord has delivered us.
Worship Father Power,
worship Mother Wisdom!

RIDDLE

Every day, every day of our lives
a beggar appears,
and as we are stretching
sleep from our limbs
he hands us a fruit
of no particular winsomeness,
a commonplace apple perhaps,
or a pear. The beggar
is a workaday commonplace beggar in rags.

Each fruit, each day, we accept,
fearful that if we refuse
the beggar will make a ruckus.

As soon as he departs
we toss each fruit out a window
where they gather in a rotting heap.

Near death, we glance out the window!
All pericarp is gone.
Instead, mounds of emeralds and rubies!
What doth this say of mortal fruits?

PRAYER, IN EXTREMITY

Lord, our lantern, our harboring,
transform our bodies' wounds,
cool our bloodied heads,
cauterize our bruises,
knead our wrenched muscles.
We tingle, loving Thee.

SNAIL

Fear tracks snail-like over the wet ledges hidden
from moon and rain. Yet, in a brilliant cascade
of flickering greed, fear slimes my mind.

We have rehung most of the doors demolished by the mob
and have repaired the chimney where the mortar and bricks
were loosened.

With din, as Hell chatters, clapping its jaws,
we honor the green flicker, that cascade, bilious—
and tranquility appears, a hue of roses. Home again!
We station brothers at the windows
to warn us of approaching evil-doers.
We pass the night dancing.

MOB

A mob waits to catch us at Enfield.
I address my followers in a forest of firs and white
birch. This takes time.

VISION

Along the grassy road
our attackers float, raging.

Their throats belch fire
through an indigo cloud.

They pass by without seeing us
where we crouch in the willows.

We move on.

As in a hurricane
they revolve backwards.

Our lives are stolen, they exclaim,
from lightning.

We shudder under their truncheons.
We bleed, singing for joy!

THE HANDSOME AMERICAN OFFICER

A dashing young American
in a black uniform,
on a jet stallion,
rears in his saddle
and plunges through the middle
of the mob surrounding
the hapless Believers.

Fists fly, whips crack
over the kneeling Shakers:

> "Our bodies are nothing.
> Our Souls are unhurtable.
> We welcome your beatings.
> See, we're comfortable
> as you lash our faces."

The officer, shielding Mother Ann, flails the mob with his whip, until they turn like wretched children and race through the forest. Then, touching his hat brim, without giving his name, he leaves on the trail whence he came.

GOSPEL TONGUES

600 persons (in 60 sleighs) hear Mother preach at Ashfield
on the first of November. Eyewitnesses, ecstatic, see
tongues of Gospel Fire burst from Mother Ann,
tongues of flame rampant in those gathered in assembly,
purifying them. Fire streams around the hall, touching
heads and tongues, firing the communicants. Peace descends on
Ashfield.

JEMIMAH WILKINSON

1.

Jemimah Wilkinson
the *Public Universal Friend*,
followed to the Millenium
Ann Lee's exordium, and
in a brash imitation
gave her soul to Christ.

2.

By means of a staged coma
she arranged herself picturesquely
in death's aroma. Then,
after a spoonful of elixir,
she fluttered her lids
and letting her pulse glow
slid up in bed
and announced she'd been dead—
now hers was a glorious show,
in perpetuo.
Though her body remained
her Soul she'd exchanged
for the *Spirit of Life Eternal.*
As the female Christ she'd returned to fight
the burns of the carnal.
She had lived and had risen again!

3.

Slender, beautiful, and twenty-three,
black-eyed, lustrous-haired, and sinewy,
she had advantages over Mother Ann Lee
who was plain, dun, and somewhat short,
whose simple dress made her look stout
and who cared not a fig for illusion or art.

Wearing her habitual male attire
and over it a flowing robe, Jemimah
on horseback packed herself all over
Connecticut and Rhode Island.
What a sight, trailing her robe
in field and shade, followed by worshippers
over hill and through glade!

4.

And she had success, scattering pearls
before men of means (she wasn't about
to sell her celestial wares for beans)
until by 1782, she'd established three
churches true, and boasted an elaborate
mansion or two, as well as a huge plantation.

These were the gifts of a wealthy
Judge Potter, who wasn't interested
in her as a daughter, or as a spiritual guide

and benefactor. Despite her beauty and her class
(or because of it) the Judge simply wanted
her ass. Could you blame him?
so passionate, raunchy, and ripe—for craving
sex with the *Spirit of Life?*

Jemimah led her judge a merry chase
to his bankers. She wangled him out of cash
and numerous acres. *Jerusalem* attracted
numerous takers.

Deluded and deprived, Judge Potter tried
the courts for justice, but lost his health
as well as the lawsuits.

5.

In *Jerusalem*, on the banks of Seneca Lake,
Miss Wilkinson waxed rich and sedate, until
ridden with dropsy and horribly disfigured,
a veritable witch—she decided that life
was a sonofabitch and had betrayed her.
And frozen in that eternal smirk
her end was royal, her end was obscene.
The *Spirit of Life* was a loathsome dream.
Dead she was, and dead remained.
Her followers, defecting, dismantled *Jerusalem.*
What a specimen of woman was Jemimah Wilkinson!

INSTRUCTIONS FOR DANCING

In dancing, each Believer acts for himself: begin
by springing about four inches up and down. Leap
so high you strike the roof joists. Effect a twist
or twirling before your feet strike the floor. Hop
on one leg towards the door, flap an arm, or arms,
as an angel flaps wings. Be a mighty cloud of
particles each agitated by a mighty wind. Tremble,
quiver, shake, sigh, cry, jump, groan, sing, dance
and turn, turn off (out) the Beast within. You are released!
The snake is writhing on the floor.
Touch him, then, quickly, tread upon his head.

THE SQUARE ORDER SHUFFLE, LEARNED BY
FATHER JOSEPH MEACHAM FROM A VISION OF
ANGELS DANCING BEFORE THE THRONE OF GOD

Three steps forward, turn, and three steps
back, setting the foot straight forward
at each end. Turn, and three steps forward
and a double step or "tip-tap." Repeat,
then shuffle the set apart once over.
Brethren form the square to the right,
sisters to the left:

> One, two, three steps,
> Foot straight at the turn,
> One, two, three steps,
> Equal length, solid pats.

> Strike the shuffle, little back,
> Make the solid sound,
> Keep the body right erect,
> With every joint unbound.

120

THE WORLD SEES

We have spied through the windows of The Square House
at Harvard, where groans, shrieks, loud yellings, incredible
laughters, singing and stamping feet—all have lately vibrated
the timbers of that house, and of adjoining ones.

What we have seen! A bedlam of chanting, yelling, trembling!
Some Shakers jerking their heads and limbs uncontrollably
for upwards of twenty minutes, others threshing around wildly
on the floor whilst others ramble around them, oblivious.

Some lie as dead (who knows for how long—it's rumored
for hours). Some are beasts and go on all fours like maddened
dogs, or whelps, barking, howling, and snapping at others
in like dismal states of mind. We have noticed, strongly,
that the men seldom mingle with the women, the latter
engendering hysteria and beast-madness, in their own parts
of the building. It is unlikely, therefore, that they are,
as rumored, licentious and libidinous.

But, of this we are certain: we are dismayed, as God-fearing
citizens, to have such madness in our midst. Certainly their
rheums, catarrhs, and effluvia let loose upon Harvard
will propel the rest of us to early graves. We shall
deal with these folk as we must, to silence them.

121

MOTHER'S FIRE

O, I love Mother's fire.
And I love the Elders' fire.
O, I love the fire dropping
from angel mouths above.

SHAKING SONG

Shake, shake as the heavenly
waters flow. Shake, shake
as they solace the earth below.
Come, Lord, as water.
Come, Lord, as flame.
Shake, shake our living forms
until we praise your name,
tipsy with your Power.
We shake and turn and tremble
until our errors crumble:

> Come, life, Shaker life
> Come, Life Eternal
> Come and shake out of us
> All that is carnal.

HERE WE STAND

Here we stand in brotherly love,
brother. Take my hand
in brotherly love, brother.

Here we stand in sisterly love,
sister. Take my hand
in sisterly love, sister.

O, it's good to be spiritual,
it's good to be free, it's
good to find the love of Eternity.
This is a splendid occasion.

MEMORIAL POEM

Whence comes this bright celestial light? What cause produces this?
A heaven opens to my sight, bright scenes of joy and bliss.

Richard Treat is horribly beaten.
Much of his cheek is flayed away.

O Lord Jehovah art Thou here? This light proclaims Thou art.
I am indeed, I'm always near unto the humble heart.

Dyer Fitch is bull-whipped repeatedly,
so that his jerkin is bloody and in shreds.
Throughout, he remains kneeling,
crying on God's help.

The proud and lofty I despise, and bless the meek and low.
I hear the humble soul that cries and comfort I bestow.

James Shepherd is placed naked
in a ring of men who beat him with birches
cut from the woods, fresh, for the purpose.
He is left supine, his back a mass of jelly.

Of all the trees among the wood I've chose one little vine.
The meek and low are Right to me—the humble heart is mine.

Mary Partington is beaten with fists,
and probed in her secret parts.
She bears scars on her face and arms
for the rest of her life.

Tall cedars fall before the wind, the tempest breaks the oak,
While slender vines will bow and bend, and rise beneath the
stroke.

William Morey has his teeth smashed
by the Captain of the mob
who has four men hold William down
while he grinds his heel
against the Believer's mouth.
With his mouth broken and bleeding
William Morey shames the mob into peace.

I've chosen me one pleasant grove and set my lovely vine,
Here in my vineyard I will rove, the humble heart is mine.

Jonathan Bridges, an old man slow in walking,
is repeatedly whipped for a quarter of a mile,
for bringing up the rear during a forced march.
The Believers are halted every mile,
over a ten mile stretch,
and men are chosen randomly, beaten, and abandoned.

Of all the fowls that beat the air I've chose one little dove.
I've made her spotless white and fair the object of my love.

Any Shaker who tries to help another
is horribly whipped.
Numerous Believers are horsewhipped
by an unknown horseman.

125

Her feathers are like purest gold. With glory she does shine.
My dove is a beauty to behold, her humble heart is mine.

Brother William Lee has his skull
cracked open, and lives for a year,
enduring severe headaches, the skull,
as is discovered after his death, never mending.

Of all the sects that fill the land—one little band I've chose,
And led them forth by my right hand and placed my love on those.

Mother Ann is pitched again into a carriage
in New Lebanon. Her cap and apron are torn off.
She is dragged twenty rods along a rough street,
behind a carriage, no mercy being shown.
Her flesh is bruised and torn considerably.
Her stomach is severely injured,
which hastens her death,
on September 8, 1784, aged 48.

She lies beside her brother William,
in the Shaker cemetery, Niskeyuna,
adjoining the Albany airport.

The lovely object of my love, around my heart shall twine,
My flock, my vineyard, and my dove, the humble heart is mine.

CODA: FOR MOTHER ANN LEE,
HER CONTINUING PRESENCE

A spirit never dies.
It kisses the lips of earth as naturally
as it flies about the skies.